Jesus Showed Us!

Written by
Bradley Jersak

Illustrated by
Shari-Anne Vis

For Eden, the marvelous mom of our children,
and Colette, my delightful, at-long-last daughter.
—Bradley Jersak

For Jeremy, Samuel, Lars, and Felix,
with great love.
— Shari-Anne Vis

What is God like? Jesus showed us!

In every gospel story, Jesus showed us what God is like, because Jesus is "God with us."

What did Jesus show us? That God is perfect love! That God loves us!

In the beginning was the Word, and the Word was with God,
and the Word was God.
—*John 1:1*

The Word became flesh, and made his dwelling among us.
We have seen his glory.
—*John 1:14*

Nobody has ever seen the Father, but the one and only Son,
who is himself God and is in closest relationship with the Father,
has made him known
—*John 1:18*

Anyone who has seen me, has seen the Father.
—*John 14*

The Son is the image of the invisible God.
— *Colossians 1:15*

For in Christ, all the fullness of God lives in Jesus in bodily form.
—*Colossians 2:9*

The Son is the radiance of God's glory,
and the exact representation of his being.
—*Hebrews 1:3*

Jesus Showed Us!

What is God like?

The answer depends on the imagination of those we ask. Some of those answers are not very healthy—especially for children! Many ideas and images of God are harmful, such as the angry God who threatens us. Or the distant God who is not there when we need him. Or the magical God who will grant our wishes if we are good enough or beg hard enough. Such ideas of God make it hard for us to love God with our whole heart or to let God love us.

God noticed this problem. God wanted us to know what God is really like. So God decided to do something. What's the best way for God to tell us what God is like? By showing us—in person! And that is exactly what God did! God came into our world as Jesus Christ. Jesus is what God has to say about Godself.

What did Jesus show us about God? **Jesus showed us that God is Love!** Not just any kind of love. God is perfect love that never stops loving. Jesus showed us this in so many ways. The four gospels, written by Matthew, Mark, Luke, and John, tell us that story. They tell us how Jesus showed us God.

Everything Jesus said and did was about this message: **God is Love.** God loves everyone, and that means **God loves you.**

Each page of this book shares the gospel story of God's love, seen in Jesus.

What is God like? Jesus showed us! Jesus showed us God is Love!

What is God like?
Jesus showed us!

Jesus said, "God is Spirit."
That means God is invisible.
How can you see God if God is invisible?

Jesus showed us!

Jesus is the picture of the invisible God!
When God looks in a mirror, what does God see?
God sees Jesus! God looks exactly like Jesus!

What is God like?
Jesus showed us!

"God is Light!" Where is God's light?
Everywhere!

"God is Love!" Where is God's love?
Everywhere!

God is everywhere and in everything!
God is not just in heaven. God is in you!
God's light and God's love are in your heart!

What is God like?
Jesus showed us!

God came to our world!
God came to live with us!

Why did God do that? Because God loves the whole world!
And God wants everyone to know God and to love God!

How did God come to our world?

Jesus showed us!

Do you remember when?
Do you remember how?

Yes, God came as a person—a very tiny person!
God came as a baby! What a great surprise!

What was the baby's name? Do you know?
Yes, the baby's name was Jesus!

The angel gave Jesus another name: Emmanuel.
What does that mean?
Emmanuel means God is with us!

Jesus is God with us!

What is God like?
Jesus showed us!

How do we know God? We look at Jesus!
All of God lived in Jesus, in his body!
That means God is just like Jesus—exactly like Jesus!

Even when Jesus was a little child?
Yes! Anyone who looked at Jesus was looking at God,
even if they didn't know it!

But they were also looking at a little child!
Jesus had to grow up, just like us,
so he could show us what God is like.

Jesus had a mother, and her name was Mary.
Do you think Jesus loved his mom? Oh yes, very much!
Do you think Mary loved Jesus? Oh yes, very much!

Jesus also had a Father, a Father in heaven.
Do you think Jesus loved his Father? Oh yes, very much!
Do you think the Father in heaven loved Jesus? Oh yes, very much!

The Father in heaven is invisible,
but if you looked at Jesus, what would you see?
That Jesus is exactly like his Father.

Jesus showed us his Father!

What is God like?
Jesus showed us!

When Jesus grew up, he was ready to show us God.
What did Jesus do first?

Jesus asked his friend, John, to baptize him in water
even though he was already clean!

When Jesus came out of the water, God was there!
Where was God?

God was there, in Jesus.
We call Jesus "God, the only Son."

God was also there in a voice.
The Voice from heaven said, "This is my Son! I love him!"
We call that Voice "God, the Father."

And God was there like a dove.
The Dove came down from heaven and rested on Jesus.
We call that Dove "God, the Holy Spirit."

Father, Son, and Holy Spirit were all there together.
Together, we call them "One God, the Holy Trinity,
always together and never apart."
Father, Son, and Holy Spirit love each other, because God is Love!

Jesus showed us!

What is God like?
Jesus showed us!

Jesus showed us that God loves children.
God loves all children—every kind of child,
everywhere in the whole wide world!

God loves children of every size—really small and really big!
God loves children of every nation and every color!
Wait! What if they were green? Yes, even if they were green!

God loves all children, whether they are rich or poor,
happy or sad, healthy or sick, serious or silly.

God loves children who love God.
But listen very carefully:
God also loves children who **don't** love God.
God loves children who **don't** even know God.
Why? Because **God is Love,** so God loves **everyone!**

Jesus said, "Let the children come to me!
All of them! I want to be their friend!
I love every one of them!"

Does God love children? Oh yes!

Jesus showed us!

**What is God like?
Jesus showed us!**

Jesus showed us that God loves everyone.
God even loves people who are different.

God loves people who live in different places,
people with different clothes and different houses,
people with different hair and different skin,
people with different music and different languages,
even people with a different faith.

When people are different, we don't need to be afraid.
God isn't afraid! God is Love!

Jesus showed us!

Once, Jesus came to a well and asked a woman for a drink of water.
She was different. She was from a different country.
She had a different family. She had a different faith.

Jesus loved her so much—as much as anyone else!
Then Jesus gave her a drink—a drink of eternal life!

God loves everyone, even people who are different!
Are you different? That means you're special! God loves you!

Jesus showed us!

What is God like?
Jesus showed us!

Jesus showed us that God cares.

God cares about people when life is hard.
God cares when people are poor or hungry, sad or tired.
God cares about people who become sick or get hurt.
God cares about people whose hearts are broken.

Jesus showed us!

Jesus showed us that God loves to heal people.
Jesus healed a man whose eyes were blind,
Jesus healed a woman whose back was crooked,
Jesus healed people who couldn't walk.

Jesus showed us that God didn't make them sick
or blind or crooked or crippled. No!
God loved them all and cared about their problems.

Jesus showed us!

One day, God's love will make everyone well!
No more problems, no more tears!

So we pray, "Lord Jesus, please come quickly!
Lots of people need your help!"

What is God like?
Jesus showed us!

Jesus showed us that God cares.

God cares about people who are poor and hungry,
people who don't have warm clothes or their own bed.

Sometimes Jesus fed thousands of hungry people.
That's because Jesus cared about them.
Jesus wanted to feed them—even when he had no food!

How did Jesus feed them? How did Jesus help them?
First, Jesus asked his friends to help him,
but they had no food either.
But one little child had some food—one little lunch.
The child shared that lunch. The child was God's helper.

Then Jesus asked God for help. He prayed.
God heard Jesus' prayer and God helped him.
God turned that little lunch into a lot of food!
Enough food for a giant crowd to eat and even some extra!

Jesus showed us!

Jesus showed us that God cares and God helps.
Jesus showed us that God's children can help too.
Would you like to be God's helper?

What is God like?
Jesus showed us!

Jesus showed us what God is like by telling amazing stories.
We call those stories parables. Do you know any parables?
Jesus told parables to show us what God is like!

One of Jesus' parables is about a boy who ran away from home.
Some people call that boy "the prodigal son."

The boy got lost, very lost, for a long time!
When the boy ran away, he ran out of food.
He ran out of money. He ran out of friends.
When the boy ran away, he got in a lot of trouble!

Was the boy's dad angry with him?
No! The dad missed his son so much!
When the boy came home, his dad was excited to see him!
The dad ran to his son and gave him a big hug!
The dad said, "I'm so happy! We need to have a party!"

Jesus said, "That's what God is like!"
Even when we run away from God's love, God always loves us!
God doesn't want us to hide or be afraid.
God wants us to run home as fast as we can.
God wants to give us a big warm hug!

Jesus showed us!

What is God like?
Jesus showed us!

Jesus showed us God's glory.
What is God's glory?
God's glory is God's love, shining like the sun!
The glory of God's love shone brightly through Jesus!

One day, Jesus took three of his friends up on a mountain.
The three friends were Peter, James, and John.
Suddenly, two more of God's friends showed up!
God's friends were Moses and Elijah.
Moses and Elijah were standing with Jesus.

And Jesus started to shine!
God's light in Jesus was brighter than the sun!
The light was God's glory. The light was God's love.
It was so bright that Peter, James, and John couldn't even stand up!

Then God the Father spoke from heaven:
"This is my Son! I love him! Listen to him!"

No one is quite like Jesus,
not Peter, James, or John, not even Moses or Elijah.
Only Jesus is exactly like God.

God showed us!

What is God like?
Jesus showed us!

On Palm Sunday, Jesus rode into Jerusalem like a king.
Jesus showed us that God is a king.
But God is not like any other king!

Most kings rule by being rich and powerful.
Some kings don't love their people.
Some kings don't care about little children.
Some kings are very mean.

God is not that kind of king. What kind of king is God?
Jesus showed us!

God is a king like Jesus!
King Jesus is humble and gentle and kind.
He rode on a little donkey, not a giant warhorse.
His followers were not mighty soldiers waving swords.
They were little children waving palm branches.
When King Jesus came, the children shouted, "Hosannah!"
Hosannah means "God, please save us!"

And God did save us! How did God save us?
Jesus showed us!

God sent King Jesus to save us with Love!

What is God like?
Jesus showed us!

Jesus showed us that God is humble and kind.
One day, Jesus took a bowl of water and a towel.
He knelt down and washed his friends' dirty, smelly feet!
Why did Jesus do that?

Jesus washed their feet to show us God is humble.
God is not just the King of Glory.
God is also the Servant of the whole world.
Jesus showed us God is the Servant-King!

Jesus showed us!

Jesus did not just pretend that God is a servant.
Jesus showed us God truly **loves** to serve people.
Jesus did not show us God is a servant for just a little while.
Jesus showed us God has **always** been a Servant.

How does God serve people?
God serves us by creating a wonderful world for us to live in.
God serves us by creating wonderful people—people just like you!
God serves us by washing us clean—even on the inside!
That's right—God creates in us a clean heart!

Jesus showed us!

What is God like?
Jesus showed us!

Jesus showed us that God welcomes us to God's table.

God's table is very special.
It starts with a bit of bread and a sip of wine.

When Jesus shared God's table with his friends one last time,
he said, "This bread is my body. This wine is my blood.
Whenever you eat the bread and drink the wine at God's table,
remember how much I love you!
All of you, come eat this bread.
All of you, come drink this wine!
Welcome to my table!"

God's table is also a banquet! A banquet of love.
After we eat the bread and drink the wine,
sometimes we also share a "love feast."
A love feast is a banquet of God's love that we all share together.
Welcome to God's love feast!

When we eat at God's table, God shares Jesus with us.
When we eat at God's table, Jesus shares God's love with us.

Jesus showed us!

What is God like?
Jesus showed us!

Jesus showed us what God is like in many ways, didn't he?
Jesus showed us God's love most of all on the Cross.

God was **in** Jesus on the Cross, showing us God's love.
What does the Cross tell us about God's love?

Jesus showed us!

On the Cross, God gave the very best gift to the whole world!
What gift did God give us?
Yes, God gave us Jesus—God's firstborn Son.
Jesus was God's great love-gift for all of us!

On the Cross, Jesus forgave everyone in the whole world.
God even forgave the people who killed Jesus!
Jesus shows us that God can forgive anybody and anything!

On the Cross, Jesus suffered with everyone who suffers.
God became a human so that God could feel what we feel.
On the Cross, Jesus shows us that God understands.

Jesus showed us God's love, even when he was dying.
Jesus never ever stopped loving.

Jesus showed us!

What is God like?
Jesus showed us!

Jesus showed us that God is alive!
When Jesus died, death could not hold him, because Jesus is God!
Jesus is Life! And Life is bigger than death!
Jesus came back from the dead!
Jesus is alive! God is alive!

Jesus showed us!

Jesus wins! Life wins! Love wins!
God wins, because Jesus died to beat death!

Jesus died so he could go into the grave and rescue those who died, even Adam and Eve! Remember them?
Jesus rose from the dead and brought them back with him!
A whole parade of people followed him! Now they are alive too!

What was the first thing Jesus said when he rose from the dead?
"Don't be afraid!"
Why not? Because Jesus is alive!
What is Jesus saying to you today? "Don't be afraid!"
Why not? Because Jesus is alive and Jesus loves you!
Now that's really good news!

Jesus showed us!

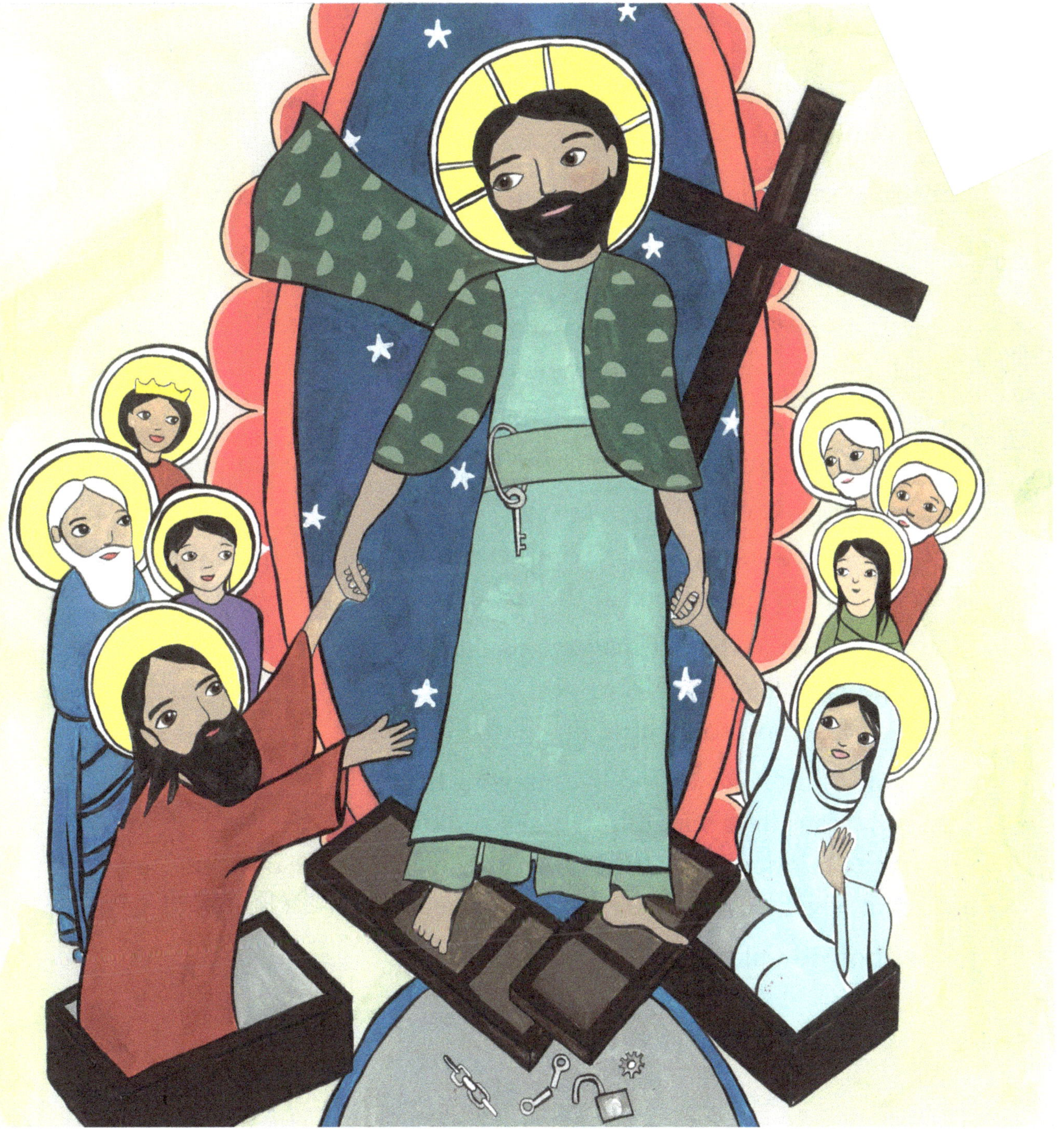

What is God like?
Jesus showed us!

Jesus rose from the dead. Now Jesus is alive forever and ever!

But why didn't Jesus stay on Earth in his body?
Sometimes I wish Jesus did stay!
But if Jesus stayed, whose house would he live in?
Would Jesus live at my house? Would you ever get a turn?

Jesus had a better idea!
Jesus said, "No line-ups! I can come live with everyone at once!"

How can Jesus do that?
Jesus can live in the house of your heart—and mine!
Jesus can live in every heart at the same time!

How can Jesus do that? Jesus gave us the Holy Spirit!
When Jesus gave us the Holy Spirit,
Jesus gave each person a little flame of God's love.

The Holy Spirit is how God lives in your heart!
And now Jesus lives with all of us, all the time!
You can talk to Jesus any time, and Jesus will always hear you!
Jesus will never leave you, because your heart is God's home!

Jesus showed us!

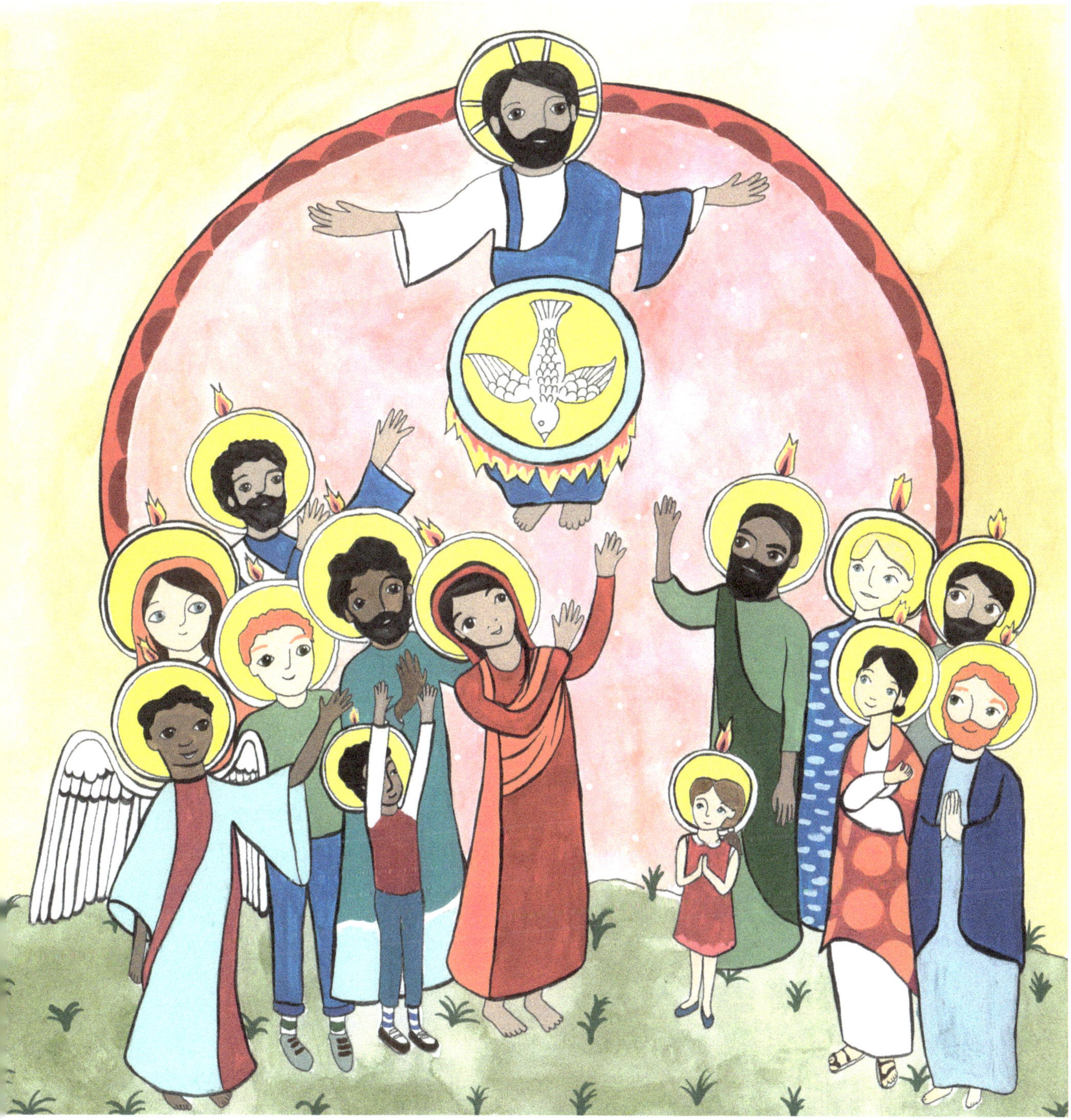

Bradley Jersak

Bradley is an author and teacher based in Abbotsford, Canada.

Even better, he's a dad! Brad and his wife, Eden, can remember how much bigger their hearts grew when their sons, Stephen, Justice, and Dominic, were born!

Most of all, Brad loves Jesus, because Jesus first loved him. What a great thing to tell children!

You can order his first children's book, *Children, Can You Hear Me?* or *A More Christlike God (Jesus Showed Us!* for adults) at bradjersak.com.

You can get coloring sheets of these pictures there, too!

Shari-Anne Vis

Born in quiet Clearbrook, BC, Shari-Anne spent her early years drawing, painting, hiking, and eating popsicles. Her life looks very similar today! In between, she travelled, earned a BFA at OCAD University, and exhibited in Canada, Italy, and Germany. She lives in Vancouver, BC, with her husband and three sons, who love Jesus, drawing, collecting seashells, and creating bunk bed parties. This is her second children's book. Prints are available at shariannevis.com.

Jesus Showed Us! © 2016 by Bradley Jersak
Illustrations © 2016 by Shari-Anne Vis

All rights reserved. No part of this publication may be reproduced, stored in a retrieval system, or transmitted in any form or by any means without prior written permission from Fresh Wind Press. Licensing of digital versions of the book for educational purposes in churches and schools is available through the publisher (freshwindpress@gmail.com).

The illustrations in "Jesus Showed Us" are inspired by Ethiopian and Coptic Orthodox iconography. They were rendered by Shari-Anne in gouache, watercolor, pencil, and ink. She gave about thirty hours of love to each piece. Quality prints of the art can be purchased through Shari-Anne Vis. Contact her at www.shariannevis.com.

Editor: Kevin Miller – kevinmillerxi@gmail.com.

All scripture quotations, are taken from the HOLY BIBLE, NEW INTERNATIONAL VERSION®. NIV®. Copyright © 1984 by International Bible Society. UBP Zondervan. All rights reserved.

St. Macrina Press
2170 Maywood Ct., Abbotsford, BC,
CANADA V2S 4Z1
E-mail: freshwindpress@gmail.com

Library and Archives Canada Cataloguing in Publication

Jersak, Brad, 1964-, author
    Jesus showed us! / author, Bradley Jersak ; illustrator, Shari-Anne Vis.

ISBN 978-1-927512-06-7 (hardback)

    1. God--Love--Juvenile literature. 2. Jesus Christ--Juvenile literature. 3. Bible stories, English--New Testament--Juvenile literature. I. Vis, Shari-Anne, illustrator II. Title.

BT140.J477 2016   j231'.6   C2016-905491-8

Printed in Canada by Friesens Corporation, Altona, Manitoba